my itty-bitty bio

Ilona Maher

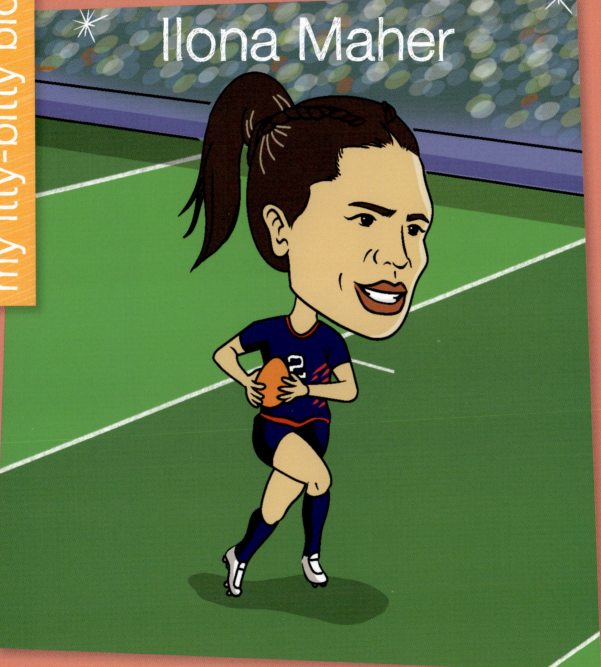

Published in the United States of America by Cherry Lake Publishing
Ann Arbor, Michigan
www.cherrylakepublishing.com

Reading Adviser: Beth Walker Gambro, MS, Ed., Reading Consultant, Yorkville, IL
Illustrator: Leo Trinidad

Photo Credits: © Sean Pavone/Shutterstock, 5; © Barabasa/Shutterstock, 7, 22; © Walter Arce/Dreamstime.com, 9; © AP Photo/Tsvangirayi Mukwazhi/ASSOCIATED PRESS, 11, 23; © UPI/Alamy Stock Photo, 13; © Martin Edwards/Alamy Stock Photo, 15; © AP Photo/Kirsty Wigglesworth/ASSOCIATED PRESS, 17; © 2024 Disney. All rights reserved. (Disney/Eric McCandless), 19; © Press Association via AP Images, 21

Copyright © 2026 by Cherry Lake Publishing
All rights reserved. No part of this book may be reproduced or utilized in
any form or by any means without written permission from the publisher.

Cherry Lake Press is an imprint of Cherry Lake Publishing Group

Library of Congress Cataloging-in-Publication Data has been filed and is available at catalog.loc.gov.

Printed in the United States of America

table of contents

My Story 4

Timeline 22

Glossary 24

Index 24

About the author: When not writing, Dr. Virginia Loh-Hagan serves as the Executive Director for AANAPISI Affairs and the APIDA Center at San Diego State University. She is also the Co-Executive Director of The Asian American Education Project. She lives in San Diego with her very tall husband and very naughty dogs.

About the illustrator: Leo Trinidad is a *New York Times* bestselling comic book artist, illustrator, and animator from Costa Rica. For more than 12 years, he's been creating content for children's books and TV shows. Leo created the first animated series ever produced in Central America and founded Rocket Cartoons, one of the most successful animation studios in Latin America. He is also the 2018 winner of the Central American Graphic Novel contest.

my story

I was born in 1996. I lived in Vermont. I played with my sisters.

We played sports.

My mother is a nurse. I also studied nursing.

I like caring for people.

What do you want to be?

My father is a dentist. He also played **rugby**. He inspired me.

I became a champion.

I played in the **Olympics**. I did this twice.

I won a medal.

I wear red lipstick when I play.
I can be pretty. I can also
be strong.

Women can do anything.

How do you stand out?

I am body **positive**. All body types are beautiful.

All body types can do amazing things.

I have many fans. I'm a **social media** star.

I uplift others.

I was on a **magazine** cover.
I danced on a show.

I like doing new things.

My legacy lives on. I'm a role model.

I support women in sports.

What would you like to ask me?

timeline

2018

1980

Born
1996

2024

2080

23

glossary

magazine (MAA-guh-zeen) printed collection of articles and pictures

Olympics (uh-LIM-piks) international sports contests held every 4 years

positive (PAH-zuh-tiv) good or hopeful

rugby (RUHG-bee) game where two teams compete to score points by carrying or kicking an oval ball over the other team's goal line

social media (SOH-shuhl MEE-dee-uh) websites and apps where people can create and share content

index

appearance, 12–14

birth, 4, 22
body positivity, 12–14

family, 4, 6, 8
fans, 16–17, 20

Olympics, 10–11

professions, 6–7

rugby, 8–15, 20–21

social media, 16

talent, 8, 10, 12, 16, 18–20
timeline, 22–23

women's sports, 10–16